CHARLOTTE ZOLOTOW
Say It!
pictures by
JAMES STEVENSON

MULBERRY BOOKS, *New York*

First Mulberry Edition, 1992.   1 2 3 4 5 6 7 8 9 10

Library of Congress Cataloging in Publication Data   Zolotow, Charlotte Shapiro, (date) Say it!
Summary: The love of a mother for her little girl permeates a walk they take together on an autumn day. [1.   Mothers
and daughters—Fiction]   I. Stevenson, James, (date)   II. Title.   PZ7.Z77Say   [E]   79-25115   ISBN 0-688-11711-2

FOR SUSAN

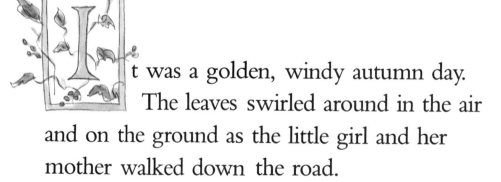

It was a golden, windy autumn day. The leaves swirled around in the air and on the ground as the little girl and her mother walked down the road.

The little girl ran ahead kicking up the leaves and then came running back and pulled at her mother's hand.

"Say it," she said. "Come on, say it!"

"It's a wild, wondrous, dazzling day," said her mother, laughing.

"No, not that," said the little girl.

Just then a small black kitten scampered down
a driveway and stood paw deep in a pool of
orange and brown leaves.

"What a black little cat you are," said the
mother. The little cat curved its paw and
went scrambling away in a scurry of leaves.
The mother and her little girl went scuffing
and scrunching around a curve.
They came to a small pond.

The wind quietened down and the
trees in the water were still. But as
they watched, the wind began again,
and the trees in the pond shivered into
a million zigzagging streaks of color.

"Look," the little girl said.

"I am," said the mother. "I'm looking."
The little girl tugged at her hand.

"Come on, say it," she said.

"It's magic," said her mother.
"It's a golden, shining, splendiferous day!"

"No," said the little girl. "That's not what
I mean."

They walked along swinging hands. The clouds were gray-purple with the sun behind. The little girl looked sidewise at her mother, waiting for her to speak.

A big dog came leaping out of the field barking at them.

"Nice boy," said the little girl, and he ran over to be patted, wagging his big tail so it swept up a spray of leaves from the ground.

"Say it," the little girl said, looking straight at her mother as their hands met in the dog's long fur.

"Nice dog, good dog," said the mother, "fine boy, what amber eyes you have!"

"No," said the little girl.

A piece of fluff from some milkweed floated by.

The little girl caught the fluff in her fingers.

"Look," she said to her mother.

"It's lovely," her mother said, "a little floating cloud full of seeds."

They walked on past a brook flowing down from the pond. It bubbled over mossy green rocks and made a muttering water sound that drowned out the crunch scrunch of their steps.

A few steps more and they came to their
own road through the meadow, and turned
up the lane leading to their house. Smoke was
coming out of the chimney, which meant the
little girl's father had made a fire to welcome
them home. Wild asters bent from side to side
in the wind. The leaves blew in swirling
circles over their heads. It blew the little girl's
hair straight up, and her mother's as well,
and made them both laugh.

The little girl ran up to her mother and flung her arms around her. The purple clouds blew into the chimney smoke, the leaves swirled around them, and the mother picked the little girl up.

"Say it," shrieked the little girl. "Say it say it say it!"

"I love you," said her mother. "I love you I love you I love you!" And she twirled around and around with the little girl in her arms until they were both dizzy.

"That's what I wanted you to say," said the little girl.

"That's what I've been saying all the time," her mother said, laughing. And she let the little girl slip gently to the ground and took her hand as they walked up the steps to their door.